THE
"DO
RIGHT"
RULES

Peter S. Chantilis, J.D.

CUSTOM PUBLISHING

60 FIFTH AVE · NEW YORK, NY · 10011

EW YORK · CHICAGO · WASHINGTON D.C. · LOS ANGELES · TORONTO

CIP Data is available.
Printed in Canada.
10 9 8 7 6 5 4 3 2 1

ISBN 0–8281–1288–6

Dedication
*This book is dedicated to my mother
Rose Chantilis. The foundation and benchmarks
in this book are her teachings.*

Contents

Table of Contents

Foreword

The "Do Right" Rules is a set of guidelines for life. Peter Chantilis, with love and compassion for his fellow man, writes from his heart and a lifetime of experience.

This book is a "quick read," but it will have long-lasting, even permanent, benefits in your life as you evaluate and ponder some of the profound statements.

In many ways the book is about relationships, because by following the suggestions and doing right, you will be able to build more stable relationships with your family, friends, and associates. That's critical because recent research by Dr. Dean Ornish indicates that the relationships and support groups in our lives are more important to our physical and mental health than diet, exercise, or even the genes we inherit.

My friends and associates in the worlds of psychiatry, psychology and the ministry assure me of the necessity of counseling in dealing with relationship difficulties—parent/child, teacher/student, employer/employee, sibling/sibling, neighbor/neighbor, etc. Mr. Chantilis has written a simple, direct, loving, and effective series of vignettes that give all of us some "rules" that will heal and avoid many of the hurts that come from relationship problems.

Peter Chantilis has struck a responsive chord by providing rules, concepts, thoughts, procedures, ideas, and wisdom that will help you build better relationships wherever you are. In our hurry-hurry, self-centered, winning-through-intimidation, looking-out-for-No.-1, me-first world, this truly is a refreshing approach.

Need I remind you that when you are getting along well with people you love, almost regardless of your financial or corporate situation, you are a reasonably happy person. On the other hand, if you're not getting along well with the important people in your life, it doesn't make any difference how much money you have or how high up on the totem pole you might be, you basically are not very happy. Here's a book that will help you in one of the most important facets of your life—building winning relationships, not only with the people you love, but also with the people you encounter in your everyday life. These "Do Right" Rules will help you live well and, more importantly, finish well.

—*Zig Ziglar, author and motivational teacher*

Preface

I have been a practicing attorney for 41 years and was involved in thousands of disputes, most of which were successfully negotiated. A few were tried at the courthouse. There is nothing like the theatre, drama, and entertainment of trying a lawsuit. As a trial lawyer for 33 years, I put on a production, as the producer, executive producer, director, scriptwriter, and wardrobe designer. My role changed for the last eight years to an attorney-mediator mediating over 1,100 disputes. Dealing with conflict has led me to several conclusions that should be helpful to you in business and personal relationships.

Several years ago I made a study of the embryonic stage or the genesis of a dispute. I mentally got up into the balcony to view the participants and their fights and discovered that what primarily got people upset was the behavior and attitude of others, specifically their temperament and tone of voice. My focus then was on suggestions and principles that should become habit in avoiding fights. *The "Do Right" Rules* is the result of this research. Doing the right thing at all times, having integrity, being ethical, being a giver, being kind and compassionate makes all the difference in avoiding conflict.

The 27 simple rules are helpful in conducting business and in maintaining personal relationships. Eleven of those rules were sent to Abigail Van Buren, who included them in her "Dear Abby" column in October of 1997, a column with a readership of 95 million. For several weeks later, there were telephone calls, faxes, and e-mails requesting permission to reproduce the rules. A Federal Judge who was speaking to lawyers on civility incorporated them in his program. *The "Do Right" Rules* became the subject matter of several speeches I have given.

Credit goes to Glen M. Ashworth, Judge of the 86th Judicial District Court, Kaufman, Texas, for his "Do Right Rule"—the inspiration for this book. In preparation for a speech on Ethics to The Kaufman County Bar Association, I needed to include the Kaufman County "local rules" of conduct in Court. Following a mediation, I conferred with Bill Conradt, Kaufman County District Attorney, and Gil Altom, a Kaufman County Attorney. They told me that although there were no written rules of Court, Judge Glen Ashworth had his "Do Right Rule." If lawyers could not get along in his Courtroom, Judge Ashworth would, on many occasions, send them out of the Courtroom with the expectation that they return after doing the right thing.

How do you know you are doing the right thing? You just know, that's all; it feels good and right. If deep down you have to ask yourself, "Is that the right thing to do?" then it probably isn't.

Doing the right thing comes naturally; it is innate, intuitive, and is a gift that you learn from your parents, your church, or from school. If you are in a position where you have a fiduciary relationship with someone and a thought comes to your mind as to whether you should disclose some remote fact or not, disclose it. If you thought about it, the chances are the other person did too; either way you should just disclose it.

Here are some reminders to help you do the right thing. They will be appreciated by the people with whom you are dealing, in both your personal and business life.

—*Peter S. Chantilis*

A PEACEMAKER SHARES SOME SUGGESTIONS

Dear Abby: I have practiced law for 40 years as a trial lawyer and counselor and have served as a mediator for more than 1,000 cases in the last seven years. In my role as a peacemaker and advocate of conflict avoidance, I have reached certain conclusions that might help your readers:

1. Learn to disagree without being disagreeable. It's all right to be assertive, but not aggressive, abusive or abrasive.

2. When someone says something with which you disagree, try not to be judgmental.

3. Maintain eye contact when greeting people, and shake their hands (Touching is important).

4. Be kind and courteous to everyone.

5. Remember that civility is a sign of strength, not weakness.

6. Speak softly (people tune out loud, angry voices).

7. Saving face is important. Give your opponent the opportunity to withdraw.

8. Your attitude is more important than your aptitude.

9. Mutual respect is the key to avoiding conflict.

10. Give the other person a chance to be heard without interrupting.

11. The shortest distance between two people is a smile.

—Peter S. Chantilis
Attorney-Mediator, Dallas
From Abigail Van Buren's
"Dear Abby" Column,
October 19, 1997

Dear Peter: Your suggestions are excellent. (My favorites are Nos. 7 and 11.)

—Abby

1

SHOW RESPECT AT ALL TIMES

Respect begins with being caring, thoughtful, gracious, kind, and courteous. You make your reputation daily. Building trust through respect enhances your ability to get along.

- Always be on time; don't be late.
- Greet your guest at the front door.
- Offer a greeting such as "Good Morning!"
- Use the person's name; the sweetest sound to everyone is his or her name.
- Offer refreshments.
- Turn off the telephone and beeper.
- Meet with people at a table rather than behind your desk.
- Dress appropriately.

Bill Walsh, former coach of the San Francisco '49ers gave his consent to The Palm Restaurant to have his caricature put on their wall, provided it would be placed next to the caricature of Tom Landry, a man he respected his whole life.

2

LISTEN TO UNDERSTAND AND LISTEN LOUDLY

When someone says something with which you disagree, do not be judgmental.

One of the most powerful experiences you can enjoy is having your communication received and understood by another non-judgmental person.

- Listen actively.
- Listen to what is being said, how it is said, and what is left unsaid.
- Understand where the other person is coming from.
- If you do not understand, do not speak, learn to listen.
- Do not interrupt: you learn by listening, not by talking.
- Keep an open mind. Listen without bias, prejudice, or predilection.
- Listen for common ground.

- You don't have to agree with what is being said.
- Perception is reality.
- Don't daydream; restrain your inner voice.
- People generally do not tell you what they want; they tell you what they think will get them what they want.

Come let us gather and reason together.

—Isaiah 1:21

3

CIVILITY

❦

Civility is a sign of strength, not weakness.

- You never have a second chance to make a first impression.
- Be polite, nice, tolerant, gracious, courteous, considerate, attentive, caring, and thoughtful.
- Maintain a great attitude and temperament.
- Avoid your passport or driver's license face.
- Would you do business with you?
- Would you hire you?

Civility is not a sign of weakness.

—John Fitzgerald Kennedy,
Inaugural Address, January 20, 1961

4

BE EMPATHETIC

Great Spirit grant that I may not criticize my
neighbors until I have walked a mile
in their moccasins.

—*Indian Prayer*

- Empathy is a great communication skill.
- Place yourself emotionally in the position of the other person.
- Listen with your eyes, ears, and heart.
- Empathy is your pain in my heart.
- Be understanding.
- Be compassionate.
- The other person knows you care when you are empathetic.

5

DEAL WITH ANGER

Conflict begins with anger.

- Be the only person who allows you to become angry.
- Be a conduit, not a sponge when you're under verbal attack.
- Separate the person (personality, persona) from the problem.
- The tone of the voice is more important than what is being said.
- Never go to bed angry with the one you love; always say "I'm sorry."
- The angry person is a disaster physiologically: heart rate is up, blood pressure is up, face is red, eyes get bigger, muscles are tight, and body is in distress.

The true object of war is peace.

—*Sun Tzu*

When angry, count to four; when very angry, swear.

—*Mark Twain*

Don't find fault. Find a remedy.

—*Henry Ford*

I never hold a grudge. As soon as I get even with the S.O.B., I forget it.

—*W.C. Fields*

I've only had two disasters in my entire life. One was when I lost a lawsuit and the other was when I won a lawsuit.

—*Voltaire*

Marriages are made in heaven ... So are thunder and lighting.

The lawmen who patrolled the prairie and quelled mass disturbances by their lonesome gave rise to the laconic motto: *TEXAS RANGERS—ONE RIOT—ONE RANGER.*

6

DISAGREE WITHOUT BEING DISAGREEABLE

Learn to disagree without being disagreeable. It's all right to be assertive, but not aggressive, abusive or abrasive.

- Learn to be an advocate. Be assertive when you are making a point, taking a position or telling a story.

- People are, in general, non-confrontational and are not looking for a fight, an argument, quarrel, disagreement or a difference of opinion.

- If you disagree with a person, make a point of saying that, with all due respect, you have a different view or perception than that person.

- Be a good wordsmith; be clear, concise, and avoid rambling or using verbal crutches such as "uh" or "ah."

- The use of "yes but" is a verbal eraser.

- Be able to separate the person from the problem.
- Learning how to disagree without being disagreeable is a skill and an art form.
- Remember the old adage "you can gather more flies with honey than with vinegar" (My mother's favorite).
- Learn to disagree agreeably.
- Learn the art of gentle persuasion and win every time.

7

BE KIND AND COURTEOUS TO EVERYONE

Don't do anything or say anything unless you mind it appearing on the front page of your daily newspaper.

Do unto others,
as you would have others do unto you.

—Matthew 7:12

My mamma always says, "If you can't say something nice about someone, don't say nothing at all."

—Thumper

Kindness gives birth to kindness.

—Sophocles

He has told you, O man, what is good;
And what does the Lord require of you
But to do Justice, to love kindness,
And to walk humbly with your God.

—Micah 6:8

When a kindness is done for another, it is also a kindness you have done for yourself.

—Benjamin Franklin

What good shall I do this day?
When you're good to others, you are best to yourself.

—Benjamin Franklin

Always do right—this will gratify some and astonish the rest.

—Mark Twain

8

SPEAK SOFTLY SO THAT ALL CAN HEAR YOU

People tune out loud, angry voices.

- A soft answer turneth away wrath.
- Shouting is a sign that you have lost control.

When I was an adjunct professor at Southern Methodist University Law School teaching "Alternative Dispute Resolution," most of the students were sitting near the back of the room. After I started speaking softly they moved to the front seats. The closer they came the more they listened.

People want to learn, but they do not necessarily want to be taught.

Wouldn't it be great if the sound volume of commercials on television and the coming attractions at the movies were not as loud and annoying?

9

SAVING FACE IS IMPORTANT

Give your opponent the opportunity to withdraw with some self-respect. The Chinese Philosopher Sun Tzu stated in the *Art of War*, "When you encircle an enemy, leave an outlet free."

- Do not embarrass the person with whom you are talking.
- When there is a difference of opinion during a confrontation and you know or believe you are right, do not ask for an admission of defeat. Do yourself a favor and enjoy a quiet victory while allowing the other person to "save face."

Several years ago I was mediating a case in East Texas, and from time to time I would say "*The Good Book* says, 'And this too shall pass,'" in the hope that I could keep the momentum going. In one of the conferences, a venerable lawyer standing in the corner who looked like Claude Rains, a movie actor in the 1940s, asked me, "Peter, where is that quote in the Bible?" I replied that I had been quoting it for years but wasn't sure of its exact source and that I'd look it up.

Looking through my Bible I discovered that the quote was not there. I tried to reach Dr. Don Benton, formerly Senior Pastor of Lovers Lane United Methodist Church, one of my co-founders of The Kindness Foundation. His daughter, in his absence, said that there was no need to look it up because it was not in the Bible, that it was William Shakespeare I had been quoting for years.

I was astonished and dismayed. After lunch I told the lawyer and all others present of the error I had made. The lawyer said, "I knew that, I just wanted you to find out, that's all."

He "had me" and could have embarrassed me, but chose not to do so. He let me off the hook, and allowed me to "save face."

Carl Sewell in his great book *Customers for Life* wrote, "try as hard as you can, you will make mistakes. As soon as they are discovered, apologize and fix the problem as soon as possible."

10

YOUR ATTITUDE IS MORE
IMPORTANT THAN YOUR APTITUDE

Your attitude controls your emotional intelligence and your ability to get along.

The beginning of most disputes is a bad attitude. I know of many disputes during business transactions and family fights in which one party spoke to the other in a manner and tone of voice that was demeaning. Both parties argued and later litigated. The lawsuits could have been easily avoided had the parties not offended each other with their attitudes.

Attitude deals with your feelings and your mood. Zig Ziglar has stated for years in his seminars and books the importance of attitude over aptitude. When I was the owner of my law firm, I took the time and responsibility to interview applicants. During the interview, I would explain that I was first looking for the chemistry between us so that we could then get into the aptitude of the person. I would set up the interview for 11:00 a.m. and the staff would take the applicant to lunch. My thought was to make sure that this person's attitude would blend and compliment that of the staff's.

To have a great attitude, you need to take several factors into consideration. You need to be polite, kind, tolerant, gracious, well-mannered, and attentive to others. Would you want to do business, or have someone in your home who was rude?

If you are of the opinion that you need to work on your attitude, what should you do? Set up a video camera or cassette player in your home or office that will record for about a couple of hours. You may be self-conscious for a short while, but you will soon forget it is there and go about your business. Later, play back the recording and make a note of negative points that you pick up. Listen or view yourself, then ask if you would want to do business with you.

Vickie Henry, the Chairman of Feedback Plus and President of Audience Connection, is known as America's Mystery Shopper. When she speaks to her audiences, she asks, "Would you do business with you?"

What face did the person you meet have on? The passport face, driver's license face, the face of a person who was having a bad day, or just his natural self?

Several years ago, I introduced my son Sam to Mr. Weldon Howell, the Chairman of the Board of Preston State Bank. He told my son that I had already made my reputation, and that Sam, at age 14, was making his reputation daily. He said that his daily behavior was important as to what people would think of him. Those statements were true then and are still true today with my son at age 37. You are on stage at all times. You are being judged by your compassion, humility, demeanor, attitude, honesty, integrity, character, and temperament.

One of the problems that you must overcome when you meet someone is acknowledging that you do have certain biases, prejudices, predilections, and conflicts. To remove all of these impediments, have an open mind and tell yourself that it is unfair to the relationship to prejudge someone. Hard to do? Yes it is, but not impossible. It takes effort, dedication, and commitment to try to keep an open mind as part of the art of gentle persuasion. You may not like the way someone looks, talks, or dresses, but you must have the right attitude to remove all that from your mind.

11

GIVE OTHERS A CHANCE TO SPEAK WITHOUT INTERRUPTION

Conversation should be a duet not a duel.

Generally, when someone is talking, you are preparing your response. You are probably thinking, "Hurry up and finish so I can tell you what I want to tell you." When that happens, you probably have not listened to all that was said. There is also a tendency to use hand gestures before you speak as if to say, "Hurry up, I already have the answer for you." Let the person finish talking, because everyone has a need to be heard. If the speaker is asking for advice, and you want to give it before he or she finishes, don't do it. Wait until you have been told the whole problem.

It is difficult not to interrupt, but it is the one thing I ask students to remember not to do when I am training. Interruptions are rude, even if the person is being obnoxious and disagreeable.

Also, be careful not to interrupt the speaker unintentionally with distractions. A lawyer observing my mediation as part of his training, had the distracting and annoying habit of jingling the change in his pocket when he got nervous. Many of us have these little distractions or ticks that we do without thinking, such as clicking your ballpoint pen, tapping your fingers on the table, tapping your feet on the floor, and shuffling papers when someone is talking.

12

THE SHORTEST DISTANCE BETWEEN TWO PEOPLE IS A SMILE AND EYE CONTACT

The eyes are the windows of the soul.

When you meet someone, look that person in the eyes. This builds trust and respect. If you are talking with someone and keep looking away, it is as if you are not telling the truth and are fearful of eye contact.

Talking with your hand in front of your mouth is a failure to communicate properly. Moreover, it causes suspicion because there is the perception that you are hiding the truth.

People like to be with happy people and a smile will do that. Think about the seven dwarfs in *Snow White* and the difference between Smiley and Grumpy. Which face would you like to view each day?

Consider the definition of "smile" in Webster's *Ninth New Collegiate Dictionary*: "a facial expression in which the eyes brighten and the corners of the mouth curve slightly upward and which expresses esp. amusement, pleasure, approval . . . a pleasant or encouraging appearance."

If you are in a retail store and there are two sales persons available, one who is smiling and the other who is not, which would you choose? There is the impression that the smiling face belongs to a pleasant and happy person of positive disposition.

When a photographer is ready to take a picture, you are asked to smile, not frown.

13

BE A GOOD WORDSMITH

> A word is not a crystal, transparent and unchanged,
> it is the skin of a living thought and may vary greatly
> in color and content according to the circumstances
> and the time in which it is used.
>
> —*Justice Holmes in* Towne v. Eisner

Do you remember the expression "Sticks and stones may break my bones, but words will never harm me?" The expression was and is not accurate. Words do hurt when they are said in a tone of voice showing displeasure or ridicule. Irrespective of the tone, some words are spoken to put you down, and to disrespect you. Verbal abuse hurts more and lasts longer than physical hurt. How often have someone's feelings been hurt by something that should not have been said?

- Avoid fighting words.
- Avoid saying, "that's not true" and say instead, "that's not accurate."

Conflict can begin with a poor choice of words. How many times have you said something you wish you hadn't, and wanted to take it back? I suspect we all have. "That's not true" is like saying "that's false," or "that's a lie," or "you are a liar." Instead, respond with an assertion that you believe the statement made is inaccurate.

We communicate by what we say, how we say it, and through body language.

14

COME IN EARLY, STAY LATE

One the best things you can do for customer service, or to enhance your relationship with your employer is to be at work early and stay late. For example, if you stop at a retail establishment to do business a few minutes before they officially open and they are ready and waiting to do business with you, you feel that they want and appreciate your business. The same thought occurs when you go by the retail establishment a few minutes after closing time and they are still there ready to do business with you. Have you ever arrived at the dry cleaners one minute after they have officially closed to find the door locked, the employees counting the money and turning off the lights, and not letting you in? How did you feel? Would you continue to do business with them?

People are not an interruption of our business. People are our business.

—Walter E. Washington,
Mayor of Washington, D.C., 1971

15

BE A GIVER, NOT A TAKER

Learn to give the edge to the other person.

There are two family members who reportedly have been fighting each other in court for years. One of the members was asked by a reporter, "what's it like being in a 50-50 partnership with your brother?" The response was "he always had to own the hyphen."

- Take a parking space further away from an entrance and leave the closer one for someone else.
- Give your place in line at a grocery store to the person who has one or two items.
- Let someone's car get in front of you, rather than cutting him or her off at an entrance ramp.
- Take some food to someone who is sick.
- Baby-sit the neighbor's kids.
- Sit with a friend who has a loved one in the hospital.

HEAR, O ISRAEL, THE LORD IS OUR GOD, THE LORD IS ONE.

Blessed be His Name and His glorious kingdom forever and ever.

SHEMA PRAYER

Thou shalt love the Lord thy God with all thy heart, and with all thy soul, and with all thy might. And these words which I command thee this day shall be upon thy heart. Thou shalt teach them diligently to thy children, speaking of them when thou sittest in thy house and when thou walkest by the way, when thou liest down and when thou risest up. Thou shalt bind them for a sign on thy hand, and they shall be as frontlets between thine eyes. And thou shalt write them upon the doorposts of thy house and upon thy gates.

—Deuteronomy 6:4–9

Aaron Klausner died November 12, 1996. He was a lay Rabbi who served Abilene's Temple Mizpah for 50 years. Abilene's Jewish Temple was built by citizens of Abilene out of respect for the hundreds of Jewish soldiers who were stationed at Camp Berkeley and had no Jewish chaplain or place to worship. Aaron began serving in 1944. He was my friend and client for more than 30 years. He was one of those rare human beings who believed a hand shake was all that was needed to confirm a deal. I asked his widow, Pearl, what prayers Aaron would have given me for this book, and the above prayers were chosen. Aaron's headstone contains the following sentiments chosen by Pearl, "A loving man who touched many lives." I dedicate this page to the memory of a benevolent man, Aaron Klausner, a dear friend.

16

ENJOY THE SIMPLE THINGS IN LIFE

- Good health.
- Take time to smell the flowers.
- There is no limit to the amount of good you can do in this world if you don't care who gets the credit.
- The sound of being alone.
- The sounds of a mockingbird or cardinal.
- Chocolate.
- Hugs, kisses, or smiles.
- A freshly cut yard.
- A rainbow and an April shower.
- Making a snowman or a snow woman.
- Having cables in the trunk when your battery dies and someone offers to help.
- Reading a great book.
- Being on stand-by and getting a seat on the last plane for the night.
- Good friends.

- Helping your grandchild put a puzzle together.
- Taking a nap and waking up.
- Putting some money in the Salvation Army's Christmas kettle.
- Having your dog or cat show you unconditional love.
- Turning the kitchen light on in the middle of the night and not seeing any cockroaches.
- Listening to your grandchild call you "grandpa," or "grandma," "yia yia," or "papou" for the first time.
- Being told daily that someone loves you.
- Being able to work.
- Reaching a gas station as you run out of gas.
- The U.S. Marine Drum & Bugle Corp.

Most Folks are about as happy as they make up their minds to be.

—*Abraham Lincoln*

Use life to provide something that outlasts it.

—*B.C. Forbes*

Honey, you ain't old until you start acting old!

—*Big Mama, Age 104*

It is better to be approximately right than to be precisely wrong.

—*Warren Edward Buffett*

May you live as long as you want to, and want to as long as you live.

—*Irish proverb*

"A Decalogue of Canons for observation in personal life"

1. Never put off till tomorrow what you can do today.
2. Never trouble another for what you can do yourself.
3. Never spend your money before you have it.
4. Never buy what you do not want because it is cheap; it will be dear to you.
5. Pride costs us more than hunger, thirst, and cold.
6. We never repent of having eaten too little.
7. Nothing is troublesome that we do willingly.
8. How much pain have cost us the evils which have never happened.
9. Take things always by their smooth handle.
10. When angry, count ten before you speak; if very angry, a hundred.

—*Thomas Jefferson*

"Desiderata"

Go placidly amid the noise and the haste, and remember what peace there may be in silence.

As far as possible, without surrender, be on good terms with all persons.

Speak your truth quietly and clearly; and listen to others, even to the dull and the ignorant; they too have their story.

Avoid loud and aggressive persons; they are vexatious to the spirit.

If you compare yourself with others, you may become vain or bitter, for always there will be greater and lesser persons than yourself.

Enjoy your achievements as well as your plans.

Keep interested in your own career, however humble; it is a real possession in the changing fortunes of time.

Exercise caution in your business affairs, for the world is full of trickery.

But let this not blind you to what virtue there is; many persons strive for high ideals, and everywhere life is full of heroism.

Be yourself.

Especially do not feign affection.

Neither be cynical about life; for in the face of all aridity and disenchantment, it is as perennial as the grass.

Take kindly the counsel of the years, gracefully surrendering the things of youth.

Nurture strength of spirit to shield you in sudden misfortune.

But do not distress yourself with dark imaginings.

Many fears are born of fatigue and loneliness.

Beyond a wholesome discipline, be gentle with yourself.

You are a child of the universe no less than the trees and the stars; you have a right to be here.

And whether or not it is clear to you, no doubt the universe is unfolding as it should.

Therefore be at peace with God, whatever you conceive Him to be.

And whatever your labors and aspirations, in the noisy confusion of life, keep peace in your soul.

With all its sham, drudgery and broken dreams, it is still a beautiful world.

Be cheerful.

Strive to be happy.

—*Max Ehrmann*

There has been confusion concerning the author of this poem. In 1956, the rector of St. Paul's Church in Baltimore, Maryland, used the poem in a collection of mimeographed inspirational material for his congregation. Someone printing it later said it was found in Old St. Paul's Church, Baltimore, dated 1692. The year 1692 is the founding date of the church and has nothing to do with the poem, which was written in 1927. It was widely distributed with the 1692 date. A copy of it was found on the bedside table of Adlai Stevenson's New York apartment after his death in 1965. He had been planning to use it on his Christmas cards, identifying it as an ancient poem. The Stevenson connection helped bring the poem to the attention of the public.

—*F.D. Cavinder*

TAKE TIME

Take time to play, it is the secret of perpetual youth.

Take time to think, it is the source of power.

Take time to be friendly, it is the road to happiness.

Take time to reach out, it is the fountain of wisdom.

Take time to laugh, it is the music of the soul.

Take time to give, it is too short a day to be selfish.

Take time to work, it is the price of success.

Take time to love, and be loved, it is a privilege.

—*provided by Susie-Melissa Cherry*

17

BE TENACIOUS, PERSISTENT, AND PERSEVERE

> Never give up; never give up,
> never, never, never give up.
>
> —*Sir Winston Churchill*

My understanding of the history of this quote is the following: Near the end of Churchill's life, he visited a school for young children. He was introduced, went to the front of the classroom and stood there for several minutes without saying anything. He then said the above words and sat down. On October 29, 1941, he gave a speech at Harrow School, "Never give in, never give in, *never, never, never, never,*—in nothing, great or small, large or petty—never give in, except to convictions of honour and good sense."

It is not the critic who counts; not the man who points out how the strong man stumbled, or where the doer of deeds could have done better. The credit belongs to the man who is actually in the arena; whose face is marred by the dust and sweat and blood; who strives valiantly; who errs and comes short again and again; who knows the great enthusiasm, the great devotions and spends himself in a worthy cause; who at the best knows in the end of the triumph of high achievement; and who at the worst, if he fails at least fails while daring greatly; so that his place shall never be with those cold and timid souls who know neither victory nor defeat.

—Theodore Roosevelt

You can let the parade walk over you, or you can jump in front and pretend it's your parade.

—Robert Strauss

If at first you don't succeed, try again. Then quit. There's no use being a damn fool about it.

—W.C. Fields

SUCCESS

To laugh often and love much, to win the respect of intelligent persons and the affection of children;

To earn the approval of honest critics and endure the betrayal of false friends;

To appreciate beauty;

To find the best in others;

To give of oneself;

To leave the world a bit better, whether by a healthy child, a garden patch or a redeemed social condition;

To have played and laughed with enthusiasm and sung with exultation;

To know even one life has breathed easier because you have lived;

This is to have succeeded!

—provided by Susie-Melissa Cherry

ENTHUSIASM

Enthusiasm is the greatest business asset in the world. It beats money, power, and influence. Single-handedly the enthusiast convinces and dominates where a small army of workers would scarcely raise a tremor of interest. Enthusiasm tramples prejudices and opposition, spurns inaction, storms the citadel of its object, and like an avalanche overwhelms and engulfs obstacles. Enthusiasm is faith in action; and faith and initiative rightly combined remove mountainous barriers and achieve the unheard of and miraculous. Set the germ of enthusiasm afloat in your business; carry it in your attitude and manner; it spreads like a contagion and influences every fiber of your industry; it begets and inspires effects you did not dream of; it means increase in production and decrease in costs; it means joy and pleasure and satisfaction to your workers; it makes life real and virile; it means spontaneous bedrock results, the vital things that pay dividends.

—provided by Susie-Melissa Cherry

18

BOY SCOUTS OF AMERICA

Here are some selected, time-honored rules or guidelines of conduct.

THE SCOUT OATH: On my honor I will do my best to do my duty to God and my country and to obey the Scout Law, to help other people at all times. To keep myself physically strong, mentally awake and morally straight.

THE SCOUT MOTTO: Be Prepared. A Scout prepares for whatever comes his way by learning all he can. He keeps himself strong, healthy, and ready to meet the challenges of life.

THE SCOUT SLOGAN: Do a Good Turn Daily. Good turns are helpful acts of kindness done quietly, without boasting, and without expecting reward or pay. Doing at least one Good Turn everyday is a normal part of a Scout's life.

SCOUT LAW

1. A Scout is TRUSTWORTHY. A Scout tells the truth. He keeps his promises. Honesty is a part of his code of conduct. People can always depend on him.

2. A Scout is LOYAL. A Scout is true to his family, friends, Scout leaders, school, nation, and world community.

3. A Scout is HELPFUL. A Scout is concerned about other people. He willingly volunteers to help others without expecting payment or reward.

4. A Scout is FRIENDLY. A Scout is a friend to all. He is a brother to other Scouts. He seeks to understand others. He respects those with ideals and customs that are different from his own.

5. A Scout is COURTEOUS. A Scout is polite to everyone regardless of age or position. He knows that good manners make it easier for people to get along together.

6. A Scout is KIND. A Scout understands there is strength in being gentle. He treats others as he wants to be treated. He does not harm or kill anything without reason.

7. A Scout is OBEDIENT. A Scout follows the rules of his family, school, and troop. He obeys the laws of his community and country. If he thinks these rules and laws are unfair, he tries to have them changed in an orderly manner rather than disobey them.

8. A Scout is CHEERFUL. A Scout looks for the bright side of life. He cheerfully does tasks that come his way. He tries to make others happy.

9. A Scout is THRIFTY. A Scout works to pay his way and to help others. He saves for the future. He protects and conserves natural resources. He carefully uses time and property.

10. A Scout is BRAVE. A Scout can face danger even if he is afraid. He has the courage to stand for what he thinks is right even if others laugh at him or threaten him.

11. A Scout is CLEAN. A Scout keeps his body and mind fit and clean. He goes around with those who believe in living by these same ideals. He helps keep his home and community clean.

12. A Scout is REVERENT. A Scout is reverent toward God. He is faithful in his religious duties. He respects the beliefs of others.

Several years ago, I was interviewing two young men to work as runners in my law firm. Both applicants were about the same, except one had achieved Eagle Scout status. I hired him due to his dedication and discipline.

Circle Ten Council Boy Scouts of America in Dallas, Texas, decided to honor the real heroes and mentors who make a difference in the lives of Scouts. They erected a monument in the center of the plaza with the following inscription: "THIS EAGLE PLAZA IS IN HONOR OF THE SCOUT MASTERS, PARENTS, AND

GUARDIANS WHO HELPED GUIDE THESE EAGLE SCOUTS
TOWARDS WORTHY MANHOOD."

The names of each Eagle Scout since 1914,
presently over 14,000 were inscribed in Texas granite
within the Eagle Plaza. These names are alphabetized
by the year, and hereafter each new class of Eagle
Scouts will be added. Less than 2% nationally of all
scouts earn Scouting's highest rank of "Eagle Scout."

19

DON'T GOSSIP OR LISTEN TO GOSSIP

If someone gossips with you about another person, do not listen, but run away. The next time they may be gossiping about you.

NOBODY'S FRIEND

My name is Gossip. I have no respect for justice.

I maim without killing. I break hearts and ruin lives.

I am cunning and malicious and gather strength with age.

The more I am quoted, the more I am believed.

My victims are helpless. They cannot protect themselves against me because I have no name and no face.

To track me down is impossible. The harder you try, the more elusive I become.

I am nobody's friend.

Once I tarnish a reputation, it is never the same.

I topple governments and wreck marriages.

I ruin careers and cause sleepless nights, heartaches and indigestion.

Even my name hisses. I am called Gossip.

I make headlines and headaches.

Before you repeat a story, ask yourself:

Is it true? Is it harmless? Is it necessary?

If it isn't, don't repeat it.

—From one of Abigail Van Buren's
"Dear Abby" Columns,
May 5, 1995

20

CONDUCT

THE BEATITUDES

Blessed are the poor in spirit: for theirs is the kingdom of heaven.

Blessed are those that mourn: for they shall be comforted.

Blessed are the meek, for they shall inherit the earth.

Blessed are those who hunger and thirst for righteousness: for they shall be satisfied.

Blessed are the merciful, for they shall obtain mercy.

Blessed are the pure in heart, for they shall see God.

Blessed are the peacemakers: for they shall be called the children of God.

Blessed are those who are persecuted for righteousness' sake, for theirs is the kingdom of heaven.

Blessed are ye, when men revile you, and persecute you, and shall utter all kinds of evil against you falsely, on my acount.

Rejoice, and be exceeding glad: for great is your reward in heaven; for so persecuted they the prophets which were before you.

—Matthew 5:3–12

THE TEN COMMANDMENTS (NOT THE TEN SUGGESTIONS)

1. "Thou shalt have no other gods before me."
2. "Thou shalt not make unto thee any graven image. . . ."
3. "Thou shalt not take the name of the LORD thy God in vain."
4. "Remember the Sabbath day, to keep holy."
5. "Honor thy father and thy mother. . . ."
6. "Thou shalt not kill."
7. "Thou shalt not commit adultery."
8. "Thou shalt not steal."
9. "Thou shalt not bear false witness against thy neighbor."
10. "Thou shalt not covet. . . ."

—Exodus 20:3–17

PROVERBS

Do not let Kindness and Truth leave you; Bind them on the tablet of your heart.

—Proverbs 3:3

ECCLESIASTES 3:
GOD'S DESIGN FOR LIFE,

He Gives Life's Order of Events

To everything there is a season and a time to every purpose under heaven;

A time to be born, and a time to die; a time to plant, and a time to pluck up that which is planted;

A time to break down, and a time to build up;

A time to kill, and a time to heal; a time to weep, and a time to mourn, and a time to dance;

A time to cast away stones, and a time to gather stones together; a time to embrace, and a time to refrain from embracing;

A time to seek, and a time to lose; a time to keep, and a time to cast away;

A time to rend, and a time to sew; a time to keep silence, and a time to speak;

A time to love, and a time to hate; a time for war, and a time of peace;

What profit hath he that worketh in that wherein he laboureth?

I have seen the travail, which God hath given to the sons of men to be exercised in it.

He hath made everything beautiful in his time: also he hath put eternity to man's mind, yet no man can find out the work that God maketh from the beginning to the end.

He Gives the Good Gifts of Life,

I know that there is no good in them but for a man to rejoice, and to do good in his life.

And also that every man should eat and drink, and enjoy the food of all his labour; it is the gift of God.

THE TEN COMMANDMENTS OF HOW TO GET ALONG WITH PEOPLE

1. Keep skid chains on your tongue; always say less than you think. Cultivate a low, persuasive voice. How you say it often counts more than what you say.

2. Make promises sparingly, and keep them faithfully, no matter what it costs.

3. Never let an opportunity pass to say a kind and encouraging word to or about somebody. Praise good work, regardless of who did it. If criticism is needed, criticize helpfully, never spitefully.

4. Be interested in others, their pursuits, their work, their homes and families. Make merry with those who rejoice; with those who weep, mourn. Let everyone you meet, however humble, feel that you regard him as a person of importance.

5. Be cheerful. Don't burden or depress those around you by dwelling on your minor aches and pains and small disappointments. Remember, everyone is carrying some kind of a load.

6. Keep an open mind. Discuss but don't argue. It is a mark of a superior mind to be able to disagree without being disagreeable.

7. Let your virtues, if you have any, speak for themselves. Refuse to talk of another's vices. Discourage gossip. It is a waste of valuable time and can be extremely destructive.

8. Be careful of another's feelings. Wit and humor at another person's expense is rarely worth it and may hurt when least expected.

9. Pay no attention to ill-natured remarks about you. Remember, the person who carried the message may not be the most accurate reporter in the world. Simply live so that nobody will believe them. Disordered nerves and bad digestion are a common cause of backbiting.

10. Don't be too anxious about the credit due you. Do your best, and be patient. Forget about yourself, and let others "remember." Success is much sweeter that way.

I was in The Library of Congress obtaining a library card and the above was on a scroll on someone's desk. Nancy Hunter and Angie told me they did not know the author and were kind enough to give me a copy for this book.

21

CITIZENSHIP

Athenian Oath:

I will not disgrace my sacred arms nor desert my
   comrade, wherever I am stationed.
I will fight for things sacred and things profane.
And both alone and with all to help me.
I will transmit my fatherland not diminished
But greater and better than before.
I will obey the ruling magistrates
Who rule reasonably
And I will observe the established laws
And whatever laws in the future
May be reasonably established.
If any person seek to overturn the laws,
Both alone and with all to help me,
I will oppose him.
I will honor the religion of my fathers,
I call to witness the Gods . . .
The borders of my fatherland,
The wheat, the barley, the vines,
And the trees of the olive and the fig.

—*Athenian Ephebic Oath*

"The true and exact text of the Athenian ephebic oath is no longer in doubt. In 1932, L'Ecole Française Athenes discovered in the ancient Athenian *deme* (township) of Archarnae a fourth-century stele on which was engraved 'in dubitable letters of stone the true, ancient, authentic and official wording of the oath.'"[1]

"Less widely known [than the Oath of Hippocrates] but of equally surpassing nobility is the ancient Athenian oath of citizenship, dating probably from 'very early time.' Later, it was adopted as the oath to be taken by *ephebi*, young men of eighteen to twenty years, enrolled in the Ephebic College established in 335–334 B.C. to implement a state supported system of military training. . . . every legitimate son of pure Athenian parentage who had reached the age of eighteen must, in order to be admitted to citizenship, be enrolled therein and undergo its two year course of rigorous training in military and civic duties and activities." At the end of the first year each *ephebus* was given a spear and a shield; after receiving these arms, the ephebi took their oath.[2]

Adaptations of the oath, with varying translations, have been used by American colleges and universities.

One of the proudest moments of my life was when my mother was naturalized as an American citizen by a Judge in Federal Court giving her the oath of allegiance to the United States of America.

---

1. Trans. Clarence A. Forbes-Fletcher Harper Swift, *The Athenian Ephebic Oath of Allegiance in American Schools and Colleges*, University of California Publications in Education, vol. 11, no. 1, p. 4 (1947)pp. 2–3.

2. *Ibid.*, pp. 1–2.

22

MAN'S BEST FRIEND

Gentlemen of the jury, the best friend a man has in this world may turn against him and become his enemy. His son or daughter whom he has reared with loving care may prove ungrateful. Those who are nearest and dearest to us—those whom we trust with our happiness and our good name—may become traitors to their faith. The money that a man has he may lose. It flies away from him, perhaps when he needs it most. A man's reputation may be sacrificed in a moment of ill-considered action. The people who are prone to fall on their knees to do us honor when success is with us may be the first to throw the stone of malice when failure settles its cloud upon our heads. The one absolute, unselfish friend that man can have in this selfish world—the one that never deserts him, the one that never proves ungrateful or treacherous—is his dog.

Gentlemen of the jury, a man's dog stands by him in prosperity and in poverty, in health and in sickness. He will sleep on the cold ground, where the wintry winds blow the snow drives fiercely, if only he can be near his master's side. He will kiss the hand that has no food to offer, he will lick the wounds and sores that encounter the roughness of the world. He guards the sleep of his pauper master as if he were a prince. When all other friends desert, he remains. When riches take wings and reputation falls to pieces he is as constant in his love as the sun in its journey through the heavens. If fortune drives the master forth an outcast in the world, friendless and homeless, the faithful dog asks no higher privilege than that of accompanying him to guard against danger, to fight against his enemies.

And when the last scene of all comes, and death takes the master in its embrace, and his body is laid away in the cold ground, no matter if all other friends pursue their way, there by his graveside will the noble dog be found, his head between his paws, his eyes sad but open in alert watchfulness, faithful and true even to death.

—*George Graham Vest*

A foxhound named Drum "was known far and near as one of the fastest and least uncertain of hunting dogs." He was shot and his owner sued for damages, $150 being the maximum allowed. The case started before a Justice of the Peace, was appealed to another court and transferred to another. It was in the final trial, in the State Circuit Court as Warrensburg, Missouri, that Vest made his speech, the peroration of which is above.

According to the recollection of Thomas T. Crittenden, counsel for the defendant and later Governor of Missouri, Vest made no reference to the evidence but confined himself to a tribute to caring affection and fidelity. "He seemed to recall from history all instances where dogs displayed intelligence and fidelity to man. He quoted more lines of history and poetry about them than I had supposed had been written. . . . It was as perfect a piece of oratory as ever was heard from pulpit or bar. Court, jury, lawyers, and audience were entranced. I looked at the jury and saw all were in tears."

—*Gustav Kobbe*

According to John F. Phillips, former law partner of Vest and a member of the House of Representatives, whose comments appear in the Congressional Record with eulogy on the dog, the jury returned a verdict for the plaintiff for $500, far more than the sum sued for. The excess was remitted. Vest was elected to the Senate eight years later and served 1870–1904.

FOUR GREAT FRIENDS!

We had four dogs that became loving members of our family. It dawned on us the other day that all their names began with the letter "M." Minky, the first and my daughter's favorite, fitted in the palm of my hand when she first came to us. Muffitt, whom I originally named Bandit because of his black and white coloring, was given to a doctor who lived close by. I anguished over letting him go.

Five years later the doctor and his family left for the Middle East and called me to see if I would take Muffitt back, which of course I did. Then there was Max who has been left at the police station looking like a wreck. My daughter and I took him home so we wound up with another great friend. Misty was left at the vet's by someone who went to New York and never claimed her back and we had another family friend. One of the most gut-wrenching experiences was the death of three of our friends. Max is still going strong. They are buried near each other at the farm. There is no experience that can duplicate the attraction, connection, love, and friendship of these four friends.

23

PATRIOTISM

❦

Place your hand over your heart when the American flag passes in a parade and when you recite the Pledge of Allegiance.

Remove your hat when the national anthem, "The Star Spangled Banner" is played.

Fly your American flag on all national holidays.

Vote in all elections.

Celebrate and honor the Fourth of July, Memorial Day and Veterans Day.

Buy a poppy from the American Legion on the 4th of July and watch the movies *1776* and *Yankee Doodle Dandy*.

I AM THE NATION

I was born on July 4, 1776, and the Declaration of Independence is my birth certificate. The bloodlines of the world run in my veins, because I offered freedom to the oppressed. I am many things, and many people. I am the nation.

I am 213 million living souls—and the ghost of millions who have lived and died for me.

I am Nathan Hale and Paul Revere. I stood at Lexington and fired the shot heard around the world. I am Washington, Jefferson and Patrick Henry. I am John Paul Jones, the Green Mountain Boys and Davy Crockett. I am Lee and Grant and Abe Lincoln.

I remember the Alamo, the Maine and Pearl Harbor. When freedom called I answered and stayed until it was over, over there. I left my heroic dead in flanders fields, on the rock of Corregidor, on the bleak slopes of Korea and in the steaming jungle of Vietnam.

I am the Brooklyn Bridge, the wheat lands of Kansas and the granite hills of Vermont. I am the coalfields of the Virginias and Pennsylvania, the fertile lands of the West, the Golden Gate and the Grand Canyon. I am Independence Hall, the Monitor and the Merrimac.

I am big. I sprawl from the Atlantic to the Pacific . . . my arms reach out to embrace Alaska and Hawaii . . . three million square miles throbbing with industry. I am more than five million farms. I am forest, field, mountain and desert. I am quiet villages—and cities that never sleep.

You can look at me and see Ben Franklin walking down the streets of Philadelphia with his breadloaf under his arm. You can see Betsy Ross with her needle. You can see the lights of Christmas, and hear the strains of "Auld Lang Syne" as the calendar turns.

I am Babe Ruth and the World Series. I am 110,000 schools and colleges, and 330,000 churches where my people worship God, as they think best. I am a ballot dropped in a box, the roar of a crowd in a stadium and the voice of a choir in a cathedral. I am an editorial in a newspaper and a letter to a Congressman.

I am Eli Whitney and Stephen Foster. I am Tom Edison, Albert Einstein and Billy Graham. I am Horace Greeley, Will Rogers and the Wright Brothers. I am George Washington Carver, Jonas Salk, and Martin Luther King.

I am Longfellow, Hariet Beecher Stowe, Walt Whitman and Thomas Paine.

Yes, I am the nation, and these are the things that I am. I was conceived in freedom and, God willing, in freedom I will spend the rest of my days.

May I possess always the integrity, the courage and the strength to keep myself unshackled, to remain a citadel of freedom and a beacon of hope to the world.

This is my wish, my goal, my prayer in this year of 1976—two hundred years after I was born.

—*Otto Whittaker*

This was originally written in 1955 as a public relations advertisement for the Norfolk and Western Railway, now the Norfolk Southern Corporation. It has been widely reprinted, generally without attribution, has been set to music, is reprinted by some newspapers every Independence Day, and has been read into the Congressional Record several times.

THE PLEDGE OF ALLEGIANCE

I PLEDGE ALLEGIANCE TO THE FLAG of the United States of America, and to the Republic for which it stands, one Nation under God, indivisible, with liberty and justice for all.

—Pledge of Allegiance to the Flag

This pledge was first used at the dedication of the World's Fair Grounds in Chicago, Illinois, on October 21, 1892, the four hundredth anniversary of the discovery of America and the first celebration of Columbus Day, which had been proclaimed by the president and made a national holiday by Congress. It was published in *The Youth's Companion*, September 8, 1892, p. 446, with this wording: "I pledge allegiance to the Flag and to the Republic for which it stands: one Nation indivisible, with Liberty and Justice for all."

No single author was named; the program bore the names of the executive committee, including the chairman, Francis Bellamy. A story in *The Youth's Companion*, December 20, 1917, p. 722, credits the authorship of the pledge to James B. Upham with the assistance of the 1892 committee, but in 1939 a scholarly committee of the United States Flag Association studied the question of authorship and "decided that to Francis Bellamy unquestionably belongs the honor and distinction of being the author of the original Pledge to the Flag."

—Margarette S. Miller

The wording of the 1892 pledge was originally the twenty-two words above, but the word "to" preceding "the Republic" was added immediately after the first celebration. The First National Flag Conference, 1923, altered the wording from "my Flag" to "the Flag of the United States of America," and the following year the Second National Flag Conference added "of America" to that phrase.

—*Margaret S. Miller*

IF I MAY I WOULD LIKE TO RECITE THE PLEDGE OF ALLEGIANCE AND GIVE YOU A DEFINITION FOR EACH WORD.

I—me, an individual, a committee of one.

Pledge—dedicate all of my worldly goods to give without self-pity.

Allegiance—my love and my devotion

To the Flag—our standard, Old Glory, a symbol of freedom. Wherever she waves, there is respect because your loyalty has given her a dignity that shouts freedom is everybody's job.

Of the United—that means that we have all come together.

States—individual communities that have united into 48 great states, 48 individual communities that have united into 48 great states, 48 individual communities with pride and dignity and prose, all divided with imaginary boundaries, yet united to a common purpose, which is love for country.

For which it stands.

One nation—meaning, so blessed by God.

Indivisible—incapable of being divided.

With liberty—which is freedom and the right of power to live one's own life without threats or fear or some sort of retaliation.

And justice—The principle or quality of dealing fairly with others.

For all—which means "it's as much your country as it is mine."

—*Red Skelton*

I only regret that I have but one life to give for my country.

—*Nathan Hale, last words before being hanged by the British as a spy, September 22, 1776*

Are you a politician asking what your country can do for you or a zealous one asking what you can do for your country? If you are the first, then you are a parasite; if the second, then you are an oasis in the desert.

—*Kahlil Gibran*

This statement appeared in an article written by Gibran in Arabic, over fifty years ago. The heading of that article can be translated either "The New Deal" or "The New Frontier" (p. 52).

The following translation was made before John F. Kennedy's 1961 inaugural address:

Are you a politician who says to himself: 'I will use my country for my own benefit'? If so, you are naught but a parasite living on the flesh of others. Or are you a devoted patriot, who whispers into the ear of his inner self: 'I love to serve my country as a faithful servant.' If so, you are an oasis in the desert, ready to quench the thirst of the wayfarer.

—*Kahlil Gibran*

And so, my fellow Americans: ask not what your country can do for you—ask what you can do for your country. My fellow citizens of the world: ask not what America will do for you but what together we can do for the freedom of man.

—*President John F. Kennedy*

This is the one of seven inscriptions carved on the walls at the gravesite of John F. Kennedy, Arlington National Cemetery.

He foreshadowed this remark earlier: "But the New Frontier of which I speak is not a set of promises—it is a set of challenges. It sums up not what I intend to offer the American people, but what I intend to ask of them."

—*Acceptance speech, Democratic National Convention, Los Angeles, California, July 15, 1960, Vital Speeches of the Day, August 1, 1960, p. 611*

COLONEL TRAVIS' LETTERS

Commandancy of the Alamo,
Bejar, Feby. 24th, 1836–

To the people of Texas &
All Americans in the World,

Fellow Citizens & Compatriots

I am besieged, by a thousand or more of the Mexicans under Santa Anna—I have sustained continued bombardment 7 cannonade for 24 hours and have not lost a man—the enemy has demanded a surrender at discretion, otherwise, the garrison are to be put to the sword, if the fort is taken—I have answered the demand with a cannon shot, & our flag still waves proudly from the walls—I shall never surrender or retreat. Then, I call on you in the name of liberty, of patriotism, & everything dear to the American character, to come to our aid, with all despatch—the enemy is receiving reinforcements daily & will no doubt increase to three or four thousand in four or five days. If this call is neglected, I am determined to sustain myself as long as possible & die like a soldier who never forgets what is due to his own honor & and that of his country—victory or death.

William Barrett Travis,
Lt. Col. Comdt.

P.S. The Lord is on our side—when the enemy appeared in sight we had not three bushels of corn—

we have since found in deserted house 80 or 90 bushels & got into the walls 20 or 30 head of Beeves—

Travis

Sunday, March 6, 1836
The President called the convention together, and informed them that He had received by express a letter from Colonel W. Barrett Travis, Commandant of the Alamo, at Bejar de San Antonio, which required the immediate action of the convention. The letter being read by the Secretary, was as follows, to wit:

Commandancy of the Alamo, Bejar,
March 3, 1836

Sir:

In the present confusion of the political authorities of the country, and in the absence of the Commander-in-Chief, I beg leave to communicate to you the situation of this garrison. You have doubtless already seen my official report of the action of the twenty-fifth ult., made that day to Gen. Sam Houston, together with the various communications heretofore sent by express, I shall confine myself to what has transpired since that date. From the twenty-fifth to the present date, the enemy have kept up a bombardment from two howitzers, (one a five and a half inch, and the other an eight inch) and a heavy cannonade from two long nine pounders, mounted on a battery on the opposite side of the river, at a distance of four hundred yards from our walls. During this period the enemy have been busily employed in encircling us with entrenched encampments on all sides, at the following distances, to wit: in Bejar, four hundred yards west; in Lavilleta, three hundred yards south; on the ditch, eight hundred yards north. Notwithstanding all this, a company of thirty-two men from Gonzales, made their way into us on the morning of the first inst. At three o'clock, and Colonel J.B. Bonham (a courier from Gonzales) got in this morning at eleven o'clock without Molestation. I have fortified this place, so that the walls are generally proof against the cannon balls; and I still continue to entrench on the inside, and strengthen the walls by throwing up the dirt. At least two hundred shells have fallen inside of our works without having injured a single man; indeed we have been so fortunate as not to lose a man from any cause, and we have killed many of the enemy. The spirits of my men are still high, although they have had much to depress them. We have contended for ten days against an enemy whose numbers are variously estimated at from fifteen hundred to six thousand men. With General Ramier Siesma and Colonel Batris, the *aid de camp* of Santa Anna, at their head. A report was circulated that Santa Anna was with the enemy, but I think it was false. A reinforcement of about one thousand men is now entering Bejar, from the west, and I think it more than probable that Santa Anna is now in town, from the rejoicing we hear. Col. Fannin is said to be on the march to this place with reinforcements, but I fear it is not true, as I have repeatedly sent to him for aid without receiving any. Col. Bonham, my special messenger, arrived at La Bahia fourteen days ago, with a request for aid; and on the arrival of the enemy in Bejar, ten days ago, I sent an express to Colonel F. which arrived at Goliad on the next day, urging him to send us reinforcements; none have yet arrived. I look to the colonies alone for aid; unless it arrives soon, I shall have to fight the enemy on his own terms. I will, however, do the best I can under the circumstances; and I feel confident that the determined valor and desperate courage, heretofore exhibited by my men, will not fail them in the last struggle; and although they may be sacrificed to the vengeance of a gothic enemy, the victory will cost the enemy so dear, it will be worse for him than a defeat. I hope your honorable body will hasten our reinforcements, ammunition, and provisions to our aid as soon as possible. We have provisions for twenty days for the men we have. Our supply of ammunition is limited. At least five hundred pounds of cannon powder, and two hundred rounds of six, nine, twelve and eighteen pound balls, ten kegs of rifle powder and a supply of lead, should be sent to the place without delay, under a sufficient guard. If these things are promptly sent, and large reinforcements are hastened to this frontier, this neighborhood will be the great and decisive ground. The power of Santa Anna is to be met here, or in the colonies; we had better meet them here than to suffer a war of devastation to rage in our settlements. A blood red banner from the church of Bejar, and in the camp above us, is token that the war is one of vengeance against rebels; they have declared us as such; demand that we should surrender at discretion, or that this Garrison should be put to the sword. Their threats have had no influence on me or my men, but to make all fight with desperation, and that high souled courage which characterizes the patriot, who is willing to die in defense of his country's liberty and his own honor. The citizens of this municipality are all the enemies except those who have joined us heretofore. We have but three Mexicans now in the fort; those who have not joined us, in this extremity, should be declared public enemies, and their property should aid in paying the expenses of war. The bearer of this will give your honorable body a statement more in detail, should he escape through the enemy's lines.

God and Texas—victory or death.

> Your obedient servant, W. Barrett Travis,
> Lieut. Col. Comm.

P.S. The enemy's troops are still arriving, and the reinforcement will probably amount to two or three thousand.

*   *   *

The siege of the Alamo began February 13, 1836, and ended in a three-hour battle on March 6, 1836.

24

BE PROUD OF YOUR KIDS

Each of you has had countless highlights in your lives with your kids. Here are some that stand out with me. I am blessed to have Sam my son and Stephanie my daughter; I love them both. We have shared enormous joy.

Sam received his Eagle and the Order of the Arrow at a Court of Honor Ceremony, Troop 70 Boy Scouts of America at University Park Grammar School. All the families were there and it was a very proud moment when they announced his name and presented him with his Eagle. Sam then gave a smaller Eagle Scout pin to his mother. Our hearts were full of love and admiration for his discipline, dedication, and commitment to achieve his goal.

Sam was attending Baylor College of Medicine in Houston. I was in Houston for business and met him at the hospital for lunch. Seeing him for the first time in his white lab coat brought tears to my eyes and a lump to my throat (my son the Doctor). I hugged and kissed him, because I couldn't find the words to express my deep emotions for the moment, other than to tell him he looked fantastic. Sam became a Reproductive Endocrinologist. I tell everyone he makes babies the new way. Sam shares with me that there is no greater joy for him than having the parents return home with their baby.

It used to be that people would ask my son, is Peter Chantilis your father? Times have changed. Now they ask me is Dr. Sam Chantilis your son? I was sitting with him at the counter at The Highland Park Pharmacy and a couple spotted him and came up and hugged him and she kissed him. She apparently had just found out she was pregnant as a result of the invitro fertilization procedure. I have been approached and have received telephone calls from many of his patients, whose comments leave my heart filled with pride and joy.

Stephanie gave me a scroll on Father's Day many years ago that was entitled "Daddy." I framed the scroll and placed it in my office.

DADDY

4 Years: My Daddy can do anything.

7 Years: My Daddy knows a lot a whole lot.

8 Years: My Daddy doesn't know quite everything.

12 Years: Oh well, naturally Father doesn't know that either.

14 Years: Father? Hopelessly old-fashioned.

21 Years: Oh, that man is out-of-date; what did you expect?

25 Years: He knows a little bit about it, but not much.

30 Years: Must find out what Dad thinks about it.

35 Years: A little patience, let's get Dad's meaning first.

50 Years: What would Dad have thought about that?

60 Years: My Dad knew literally everything.

65 Years: I wish I could talk it over with Dad once more.

Love, Stephanie

I am an attorney-mediator and meet many attorneys and their clients. They began asking me for copies of the scroll and I have made stacks of them over the years, which are given to them.

Throughout the years people have shared with me the impact that the sentiments above have had on them. One person told me that he and his father had a very strained relationship. He sent the sentiments to his father who called him and started talking and crying and they resolved their differences. Another friend called me recently and told me that he had seen the above sentiments in *The Dallas Morning News* when the newspaper published it on Father's Day '97. He started reading it to his children on that Father's Day following his open-heart surgery and he started crying halfway through it and one of his sons finished reading it. It was an emotional moment for them. These sentiments have been shared by many, many more much to their pleasure and joy.

Stephanie became a dynamic businesswoman. After working for a travel agency, she bought a franchise from scratch called "Cookie Bouquet." She negotiated a franchise, found a storefront and leased it in Snider Plaza, bought her equipment and furnishings and started in the cookie business all by herself. I was so proud of her to accomplish all that without any help. She allowed me to become part of her delivery service on her busiest day of the year, Valentine's Day.

She kept the franchise for five years and sold it for a nice profit after she got married. She now has two beautiful children and I am a very proud grandfather.

25

MAKE, SPEND, AND HAVE

Do the right thing for your family and yourself, by saving 10% of everything you earn. Invest that 10% and it will double dramatically in your lifetime. The miracle of compound interest takes over and you will ultimately be a rich person. There is an old definition that "a rich person is one who can live off of the income of his investments."

Compound interest is extraordinary. It is based on the Rule of 72. Divide the interest rate you earn into 72 and that will tell you the number of years needed to double your investment. As an example, if you earn 6%, 72 ÷ 6 = 12, so your investment will double in 12 years.

My father and mother had a third grade education obtained from a small school in a village of 700 in Andretsena, Olympia, Greece. They figured you ought to be able to live comfortably on 90% of your income.

We lived during the depression when there was practically no money, no jobs, plenty of soup lines. They saved whatever they could get their hands on.

If you ever decide to guarantee some debt, don't violate the Cardinal Rule of the Rich by guaranteeing your entire net worth. Many did that in the early '80s and there was much regret when we went through a bank, oil, and real estate depression in the mid '80s.

26

ETHICS, TRUTH, HONESTY, INTEGRITY, AND CHARACTER

- Tell the truth at all times.
- Be honest with everyone.
- Uphold the highest integrity.
- Be of the highest moral and ethical strength.
- Be the best you can be.
- Do the right thing.

There are lies, damn lies, and statistics.

—*Mark Twain*

Do that which is good and no evil shall touch you.

—*Tobit*

I believe that truth is the glue that holds government together, not only our government but civilization itself. That bond, though strained, is unbroken at home and abroad.

—*President Gerald R. Ford,*
remarks upon taking the Oath of Office, August 9, 1974

Charles M. Schwab, Chairman of Bethlehem Steel, one of the largest independent steel companies in America died broke.

Samuel Insull, Chairman of Commonwealth Edison Company and other utility corporations, was acquitted on embezzlement and mail fraud charges. He died in Paris in modest surroundings.

Howard Hopson, President of Associated Gas & Electric Utility Empire, had been in prison for mail fraud charges and died in a sanitarium.

Richard Whitney, President of New York Stock Exchange, served time in Sing-Sing for grand larceny.

Albert Fall, Secretary of the Interior in Harding's Cabinet, served a prison term for accepting a bribe.

When a man assumes a public trust, he should consider himself a public property.

Speaking at a White House dinner for sixteen Nobel Prize winners, President John F. Kennedy said: "Surely this is the most intellectual gathering ever, except when Thomas Jefferson dined alone."

Honesty is the first chapter in the Book of Wisdom. Let it be our endeavor to merit the character of a just nation.

—*Thomas Jefferson*

You never get mixed up if you simply tell the truth. Then you don't have to remember what you have said, and you never forget what you have said.

—*Representative Sam Rayburn*

27

HUMAN RELATIONSHIPS

In human relationships there is none more important than *The Golden Rule*:

"Do unto others
as you would have them do unto you."

Also, the first part of *Ephesians* 4:32:

"Be ye kind one to another, tenderhearted, forgiving each other."

Perhaps, most important, the verses *Matthew* 22:37–39:

"You must love the Lord your God with all your heart, with all your soul, and with all your mind. This is the first and greatest commandment. A second is like unto it: Love your neighbor as yourself."

Those are strong quotes from the Bible, and the neat thing is they work in everyday life.

—Zig Ziglar, author and motivational teacher

Bibliography

Archives Division, Texas State Library and Archives Commission, Austin, Texas.

Boy Scouts of America, *Boy Scout Handbook*, 1988.

Buffet, Warren Edward, *Fortune* Magazine, April 4, 1994.

Cavinder, F.D., "Desiderata," *TWA Ambassador*, pp. 14–15, August 1973.

Congressional Research Service, *Respectfully Quoted*, A Dictionary of Quotations, Washington, D.C., 1989.

Churchill, Winston S., *His Complete Speeches, 1897–1963*, ed. Robert Rhodes James, Vol. 6, p. 6499 (1974).

Disney, Walt, *Bambi*, 1942.

Ehrmann, Max, "Desiderata," *The Poems of Max Ehrmann*, p. 165 (1948).

Forbes, Clarence A., trans. *The Athenian Ephebic Oath of Allegiance in American Schools and Colleges*, University of California Publications in Education, vol. 11, no. 1, p. 1–4, 1947.

Ford, Gerald R., *Public Papers of the Presidents of the United States*, 1974, p. 2.

Gibran, Kahlil, *A Third Treasury of Kahlil Gibran*, ed. Andrew Dib Sherfan, p. 53.

Gibran, Kahlil, *The Voice of the Master*, trans. Anthony R. Ferris, p. 34, 1958.

Henry, Vicki, *Feedback on Calls*, Feedback Plus, Inc., 1998.

Himmelfarb, Gertrude, ed. *Essays on Freedom and Power*, Lord Acton Letter to Mandell Creighton, April 5, 1887, pp. 335–6, 1972.

Jefferson, Thomas, *Writings of Thomas Jefferson*, letter to Thomas Jefferson Smith, February 21, 1825, ed. Paul L. Ford vol. 10, p. 341, 1899.

Kennedy, John F., *Inaugural Addresses of the Presidents of the United States*. US Government Printing Office, Washington, DC, 1989.

Kobbe, Gustav, *A Tribute to the Dog*, pp. 9–18, 1911.

Laws of Texas, Vol. I, The Gammel Book Company, pp. 25–26, 1898.

Merriam Webster Inc., ed. *Webster's Ninth New Collegiate Dictionary*, 1988.

Miller, Margaret, *I Pledge Allegiance*, Congressional Record, vol. 118, p. 20859, Flag Day, June 14, 1972.

Moody Press, ed. *New American Standard Bible*, 1975.

Rayburn, Sam, Representative, private conversation. Ragsdale, W.B., "An Old Friend Writes of Rayburn," *U.S. News and World Report*, October 23, 1961, p. 72.

Roosevelt, Theodore, *The Works of Theodore*

Roosevelt, "Citizenship in a Republic, the Strenuous Life," Address at the Sorbonne, Paris, France, April 23, 1910, vol. 13, ch. 21, p. 510, 1926.

Skeleton, Red, *I Pledge Allegiance*, Congressional Record, vol. 118, p. 20859, Flag Day, June 14, 1972.

Sun Tzu, *Art of War*, ed. and with Forward by James Clavell, Dell Publishing, p. 7, 1983.

Towne v. Eisner, 245 U.S. 418, 425, 1918.

Twain, Mark, A Message to the Young People's Society, Greenpoint Presbyterian Church, Brooklyn, New York, February 16, 1901.

Twain, Mark, "Pudd'nhead Wilson's Calendar," *Pudd'nhead Wilson*, 1894.

Van Buren, Abigail, "Dear Abby Column," Universal Press Syndicate.

Vest, George Graham, "Eulogy on the Dog," speech during lawsuit, *1870 Congressional Record*, October 16, 1914, vol. 51, Appendix, pp. 1235–36.

Whittaker, Otto, "I Am the Nation," *Norfolk and Western Railway Company Magazine*, January 15, 1976.

Ziglar, Zig, letter to Peter S. Chantilis, October 6, 1998.

Every attempt has been made to give proper credit for all statements made by third parties. In the event that I have not given proper credit due, please let me know and it will be corrected in the next printing.

Please send me a story that is either unusual, inspirational, humorous, heart-warming, or that deals with survival to be considered as part of my next book.

Peter S. Chantilis
200 Crescent Court
Suite #1070
Dallas, TX 75201–7836
Fax: 214.871.5101
Email: ChantilisP@aol.com
www.chantilis.com